50 Rare Spices of Indian Ocean Recipes

By: Kelly Johnson

Table of Contents

- Zanzibar Clove-Spiced Lamb Stew
- Madagascar Vanilla Bean Prawn Curry
- Comorian Ylang-Ylang Chicken
- Mauritian Nutmeg-Rubbed Grilled Fish
- Sri Lankan Cinnamon & Cardamom Rice
- Seychellois Star Anise Coconut Soup
- Malagasy Wild Pepper Beef Stir-Fry
- Goan Kokum-Infused Fish Curry
- Mascarene Island Turmeric-Spiced Vegetables
- Black Lemongrass & Tamarind Seafood Stew
- Andaman Long Pepper Crab Masala
- Maldivian Mace-Scented Tuna Salad
- Kerala Black Cardamom Duck Roast
- Pondicherry Green Cardamom Chai Custard
- Reunion Island Pink Peppercorn Lobster
- Ceylonese Coriander & Clove Rice Pilaf
- Madagascar Bourbon Vanilla Chicken Skewers
- Mauritian Masala Spiced Lentil Soup
- Zanzibar Nutmeg & Ginger Beef Kebabs
- Seychellois Curcuma Coconut Curry
- Tamil Nadu Fennel & Fenugreek Eggplant Stew
- Bourbon Vanilla & Clove-Spiced Duck Confit
- Andaman Islands Bay Leaf-Infused Seafood Broth
- Malabar Tamarind & Cinnamon Fish Fry
- Mauritian Saffron Butter Chicken
- Black Mustard & Curry Leaf Shrimp
- Kachampuli Vinegar & Star Anise Pork Curry
- Madagascar Pink Salt Crusted Red Snapper
- Seychelles Ginger & Kaffir Lime Prawn Skewers
- Maldivian Moringa-Spiced Rice Cakes
- Pondicherry Aniseed & Cumin Lamb Stew
- Kerala Wild Turmeric Mashed Yams
- Spiced Breadfruit Curry with Clove & Nutmeg
- Mascarene Island Cinnamon Sugar Plantains
- Black Lemongrass & Coconut Milk Soup

- Sri Lankan Ceylon Pepper-Crusted Chicken
- Goan Kokum & Clove Pickled Fish
- Comorian Ginger & Nutmeg Banana Fritters
- Zanzibar Cinnamon & Mace Rice Pudding
- Mauritian Fennel Seed & Saffron Lamb Curry
- Maldivian Pandan & Coconut Ice Cream
- Sri Lankan Tamarind & Aniseed Spiced Chutney
- Kerala Black Sesame & Jaggery Sweet Porridge
- Mascarene Island Vanilla Bean & Clove Cake
- Andaman Islands Smoked Cumin & Cardamom Tea
- Pondicherry Bay Leaf & Nutmeg Chicken Biryani
- Reunion Island Star Anise & Lemongrass Sorbet
- Mauritian Pink Pepper & Papaya Salad
- Zanzibar Cardamom & Clove-Spiced Mango Lassi
- Madagascar Vanilla & Cinnamon-Scented Roast Duck

Zanzibar Clove-Spiced Lamb Stew

Ingredients:

- 1 lb lamb, cubed
- 1 onion, chopped
- 3 garlic cloves, minced
- 1-inch ginger, grated
- 1 tbsp ground cloves
- 1 tsp cumin
- 1 tsp cinnamon
- 1 cup diced tomatoes
- 1 cup coconut milk
- 1/2 cup water
- 2 tbsp vegetable oil

Instructions:

1. Heat oil in a pot and brown lamb. Remove and set aside.
2. Sauté onion, garlic, and ginger until fragrant.
3. Stir in cloves, cumin, and cinnamon.
4. Add tomatoes, coconut milk, and water. Simmer for 1.5 hours.

Madagascar Vanilla Bean Prawn Curry

Ingredients:

- 1 lb prawns, peeled
- 1 vanilla bean, split and scraped
- 1 onion, sliced
- 2 garlic cloves, minced
- 1 tsp turmeric
- 1 tsp chili powder
- 1 cup coconut milk
- 1 tbsp lime juice
- 2 tbsp butter

Instructions:

1. Sauté onion and garlic in butter.
2. Stir in turmeric, chili, and vanilla seeds.
3. Add prawns, cook for 3 minutes.
4. Pour in coconut milk and simmer for 5 minutes.
5. Finish with lime juice.

Comorian Ylang-Ylang Chicken

Ingredients:

- 1 lb chicken thighs
- 1 tbsp ylang-ylang essence (or orange blossom water)
- 1 onion, chopped
- 1 tsp coriander
- 1 tsp black pepper
- 1 cup coconut milk
- 2 tbsp lemon juice

Instructions:

1. Marinate chicken in ylang-ylang, lemon juice, and spices for 1 hour.
2. Sauté onion in oil, add chicken, and brown.
3. Pour in coconut milk and simmer for 30 minutes.

Mauritian Nutmeg-Rubbed Grilled Fish

Ingredients:

- 2 fish fillets (snapper or sea bass)
- 1 tsp ground nutmeg
- 1/2 tsp salt
- 1/2 tsp black pepper
- 1 tbsp olive oil
- Juice of 1 lime

Instructions:

1. Rub fish with nutmeg, salt, and pepper.
2. Drizzle with olive oil and grill for 4 minutes per side.
3. Squeeze lime juice over before serving.

Sri Lankan Cinnamon & Cardamom Rice

Ingredients:

- 1 cup basmati rice
- 2 cinnamon sticks
- 4 cardamom pods, crushed
- 2 tbsp ghee
- 1 3/4 cups water

Instructions:

1. Heat ghee in a pot and toast cinnamon and cardamom.
2. Add rice and coat with spices.
3. Pour in water, bring to a boil, then cover and simmer for 15 minutes.

Seychellois Star Anise Coconut Soup

Ingredients:

- 1 cup coconut milk
- 2 cups vegetable broth
- 2 star anise pods
- 1-inch ginger, sliced
- 1 tbsp fish sauce (optional)
- 1 cup shrimp or tofu
- 1 lime, juiced

Instructions:

1. Simmer coconut milk, broth, star anise, and ginger for 10 minutes.
2. Add shrimp or tofu and cook for 5 minutes.
3. Stir in fish sauce and lime juice.

Malagasy Wild Pepper Beef Stir-Fry

Ingredients:

- 1 lb beef strips
- 1 tbsp wild Malagasy pepper (or black pepper)
- 1 onion, sliced
- 2 garlic cloves, minced
- 2 tbsp soy sauce
- 1 tbsp honey
- 2 tbsp oil

Instructions:

1. Heat oil and stir-fry beef for 3 minutes. Remove.
2. Sauté onion and garlic, then return beef.
3. Add pepper, soy sauce, and honey. Toss and serve.

Goan Kokum-Infused Fish Curry

Ingredients:

- 2 fish fillets
- 4 kokum petals (or tamarind paste)
- 1 onion, chopped
- 2 garlic cloves, minced
- 1 tsp cumin
- 1 tsp turmeric
- 1 cup coconut milk
- 1/2 cup water

Instructions:

1. Sauté onion and garlic in oil.
2. Stir in cumin and turmeric.
3. Add fish, kokum, coconut milk, and water. Simmer for 10 minutes.

Mascarene Island Turmeric-Spiced Vegetables

Ingredients:

- 1 zucchini, chopped
- 1 carrot, sliced
- 1 bell pepper, sliced
- 1 tsp turmeric
- 1/2 tsp cumin
- 2 tbsp coconut oil

Instructions:

1. Heat oil and stir-fry vegetables for 5 minutes.
2. Add turmeric and cumin, toss to coat.

Black Lemongrass & Tamarind Seafood Stew

Ingredients:

- 1 lb mixed seafood (shrimp, fish, mussels)
- 2 stalks lemongrass, bruised
- 1 tbsp black garlic paste
- 2 tbsp tamarind paste
- 1 onion, chopped
- 3 garlic cloves, minced
- 1 tsp smoked paprika
- 1 tsp turmeric
- 1 cup coconut milk
- 2 cups fish stock

Instructions:

1. Sauté onion, garlic, and lemongrass in oil.
2. Stir in tamarind paste, black garlic, turmeric, and paprika.
3. Pour in stock and coconut milk. Simmer for 10 minutes.
4. Add seafood and cook for 5-7 minutes.

Andaman Long Pepper Crab Masala

Ingredients:

- 2 crabs, cleaned and cracked
- 2 tbsp Andaman long pepper, crushed (or substitute black pepper)
- 1 onion, finely chopped
- 2 garlic cloves, minced
- 1 tsp cumin
- 1 tsp turmeric
- 1 tbsp tamarind pulp
- 1 cup coconut milk

Instructions:

1. Heat oil and sauté onion and garlic.
2. Add long pepper, cumin, and turmeric. Stir for 1 minute.
3. Add tamarind pulp and coconut milk.
4. Simmer crabs in sauce for 15 minutes.

Maldivian Mace-Scented Tuna Salad

Ingredients:

- 1 lb fresh tuna, seared and flaked
- 1/2 tsp ground mace
- 1 tbsp lime juice
- 1 small red onion, diced
- 1 green chili, chopped
- 1 tbsp coconut oil
- 1/2 cup grated coconut

Instructions:

1. Mix tuna with lime juice, mace, and coconut.
2. Sauté onion and chili in oil, then mix in tuna.

Kerala Black Cardamom Duck Roast

Ingredients:

- 2 duck legs
- 2 black cardamom pods, crushed
- 1 tsp cinnamon
- 1 tsp garam masala
- 1 tbsp ginger-garlic paste
- 1 cup coconut milk
- 1 tbsp vinegar

Instructions:

1. Marinate duck with spices and vinegar for 2 hours.
2. Roast at 375°F (190°C) for 1 hour, basting with coconut milk.

Pondicherry Green Cardamom Chai Custard

Ingredients:

- 2 cups milk
- 4 egg yolks
- 1/2 cup sugar
- 4 green cardamom pods, crushed
- 1 cinnamon stick
- 1 tsp black tea leaves

Instructions:

1. Simmer milk with cardamom, cinnamon, and tea leaves.
2. Strain and whisk into egg yolks and sugar.
3. Bake at 325°F (160°C) in a water bath for 30 minutes.

Reunion Island Pink Peppercorn Lobster

Ingredients:

- 2 lobster tails
- 1 tbsp crushed pink peppercorns
- 2 tbsp butter
- 1 tsp lemon zest
- 1/2 cup white wine

Instructions:

1. Sauté lobster in butter with pink peppercorns.
2. Deglaze with white wine and finish with lemon zest.

Ceylonese Coriander & Clove Rice Pilaf

Ingredients:

- 1 cup basmati rice
- 1 tsp coriander seeds, crushed
- 2 cloves
- 1 cinnamon stick
- 1 tbsp ghee
- 2 cups water

Instructions:

1. Sauté spices in ghee.
2. Add rice and water. Simmer for 15 minutes.

Madagascar Bourbon Vanilla Chicken Skewers

Ingredients:

- 1 lb chicken thighs, cubed
- 1 vanilla bean, split and scraped
- 2 tbsp honey
- 1 tbsp soy sauce
- 1 tbsp lime juice

Instructions:

1. Marinate chicken in vanilla, honey, soy sauce, and lime for 2 hours.
2. Grill skewers for 10 minutes.

Mauritian Masala Spiced Lentil Soup

Ingredients:

- 1 cup red lentils
- 1 onion, chopped
- 2 garlic cloves, minced
- 1 tsp masala spice mix
- 1/2 tsp turmeric
- 4 cups vegetable broth

Instructions:

1. Sauté onion and garlic in oil.
2. Stir in spices, then add lentils and broth.
3. Simmer for 30 minutes.

Zanzibar Nutmeg & Ginger Beef Kebabs

Ingredients:

- 1 lb beef, cubed
- 1 tsp nutmeg
- 1 tbsp grated ginger
- 1 tbsp lime juice
- 2 tbsp olive oil

Instructions:

1. Marinate beef in spices and lime for 1 hour.
2. Grill skewers for 8 minutes.

Seychellois Curcuma Coconut Curry

Ingredients:

- 1 lb chicken or vegetables (your choice)
- 1 tbsp turmeric (curcuma)
- 1 onion, chopped
- 2 garlic cloves, minced
- 1 tbsp ginger, grated
- 1 tsp cumin
- 1 tsp coriander powder
- 1 cup coconut milk
- 1 tbsp lime juice
- 2 tbsp coconut oil

Instructions:

1. Sauté onion, garlic, and ginger in coconut oil.
2. Add turmeric, cumin, and coriander. Stir for 1 minute.
3. Add chicken or vegetables and cook until browned.
4. Pour in coconut milk and simmer for 15 minutes.
5. Finish with lime juice.

Tamil Nadu Fennel & Fenugreek Eggplant Stew

Ingredients:

- 2 large eggplants, cubed
- 1 tsp fennel seeds
- 1 tsp fenugreek seeds
- 1 onion, finely chopped
- 3 garlic cloves, minced
- 1 tsp chili powder
- 1 tsp tamarind paste
- 2 tomatoes, chopped
- 1 cup coconut milk

Instructions:

1. Dry toast fennel and fenugreek seeds, then crush.
2. Sauté onion, garlic, and spices.
3. Add eggplant, tamarind, and tomatoes.
4. Pour in coconut milk and simmer for 20 minutes.

Bourbon Vanilla & Clove-Spiced Duck Confit

Ingredients:

- 2 duck legs
- 1 vanilla bean, split and scraped
- 3 cloves, crushed
- 1 tsp cinnamon
- 1 tbsp salt
- 1 tsp black pepper
- 1 cup duck fat

Instructions:

1. Rub duck legs with vanilla, cloves, cinnamon, salt, and pepper.
2. Let marinate overnight.
3. Submerge in duck fat and cook at 250°F (120°C) for 3 hours.

Andaman Islands Bay Leaf-Infused Seafood Broth

Ingredients:

- 1 lb mixed seafood (fish, shrimp, mussels)
- 3 dried bay leaves
- 1 onion, chopped
- 2 garlic cloves, minced
- 1 tsp turmeric
- 1 tsp black pepper
- 4 cups fish stock
- 1 tbsp lime juice

Instructions:

1. Sauté onion and garlic, then add bay leaves and spices.
2. Pour in fish stock and simmer for 15 minutes.
3. Add seafood and cook for 5 minutes.
4. Finish with lime juice.

Malabar Tamarind & Cinnamon Fish Fry

Ingredients:

- 4 fish fillets
- 1 tbsp tamarind paste
- 1/2 tsp cinnamon
- 1 tsp turmeric
- 1 tsp red chili powder
- 2 tbsp rice flour
- Oil for frying

Instructions:

1. Marinate fish with tamarind, cinnamon, turmeric, and chili powder for 30 minutes.
2. Coat with rice flour.
3. Shallow fry until golden brown.

Mauritian Saffron Butter Chicken

Ingredients:

- 1 lb chicken, cubed
- 1/2 tsp saffron, soaked in 2 tbsp warm milk
- 1 onion, chopped
- 2 garlic cloves, minced
- 1 tsp garam masala
- 1 tsp turmeric
- 1 cup tomato purée
- 1/2 cup heavy cream
- 2 tbsp butter

Instructions:

1. Sauté onion, garlic, and spices in butter.
2. Add chicken and brown.
3. Stir in tomato purée and saffron milk.
4. Simmer for 15 minutes, then finish with cream.

Black Mustard & Curry Leaf Shrimp

Ingredients:

- 1 lb shrimp, cleaned
- 1 tbsp black mustard seeds
- 10 curry leaves
- 1 onion, sliced
- 2 garlic cloves, minced
- 1 tsp turmeric
- 1 tsp chili flakes
- 1 tbsp coconut oil

Instructions:

1. Heat oil and fry mustard seeds until they pop.
2. Add curry leaves, onion, and garlic.
3. Stir in turmeric and chili flakes.
4. Add shrimp and cook for 5 minutes.

Kachampuli Vinegar & Star Anise Pork Curry

Ingredients:

- 1 lb pork, cubed
- 1 tbsp kachampuli vinegar (or balsamic vinegar)
- 2 star anise
- 1 onion, chopped
- 3 garlic cloves, minced
- 1 tsp cumin
- 1 tsp black pepper
- 1 cup coconut milk

Instructions:

1. Sauté onion, garlic, and spices.
2. Add pork and brown.
3. Pour in vinegar and coconut milk.
4. Simmer for 45 minutes.

Madagascar Pink Salt Crusted Red Snapper

Ingredients:

- 1 whole red snapper
- 2 cups coarse pink salt
- 2 egg whites
- 1 lemon, sliced
- 2 sprigs thyme

Instructions:

1. Mix salt and egg whites.
2. Stuff fish with lemon and thyme.
3. Pack in salt crust and bake at 375°F (190°C) for 30 minutes.

Seychelles Ginger & Kaffir Lime Prawn Skewers

Ingredients:

- 1 lb prawns, peeled
- 1 tbsp grated ginger
- 2 kaffir lime leaves, finely chopped
- 1 tbsp soy sauce
- 1 tbsp honey

Instructions:

1. Marinate prawns for 30 minutes.
2. Thread onto skewers and grill for 5 minutes.

Maldivian Moringa-Spiced Rice Cakes

Ingredients:

- 1 cup rice flour
- 1 tbsp moringa powder
- 1/2 cup coconut milk
- 1 tsp salt

Instructions:

1. Mix all ingredients into a batter.
2. Steam for 15 minutes.

Pondicherry Aniseed & Cumin Lamb Stew

Ingredients:

- 1.5 lb lamb, cubed
- 1 tsp aniseed
- 1 tsp cumin seeds
- 1 onion, finely chopped
- 3 garlic cloves, minced
- 1 tbsp tomato paste
- 1 tsp turmeric
- 1 tsp coriander powder
- 1 cup beef broth
- 1 tbsp ghee

Instructions:

1. Toast aniseed and cumin seeds, then grind.
2. Sauté onion and garlic in ghee.
3. Add lamb, tomato paste, and spices.
4. Pour in broth and simmer for 1.5 hours.

Kerala Wild Turmeric Mashed Yams

Ingredients:

- 2 large yams, peeled and cubed
- 1 tsp wild turmeric
- 1 tbsp coconut oil
- 2 tbsp coconut milk
- 1 tsp black pepper
- Salt to taste

Instructions:

1. Boil yams until tender, then mash.
2. Mix in turmeric, coconut oil, and coconut milk.
3. Season with black pepper and salt.

Spiced Breadfruit Curry with Clove & Nutmeg

Ingredients:

- 1 medium breadfruit, peeled and cubed
- 1 onion, chopped
- 2 garlic cloves, minced
- 1 tsp cloves, crushed
- 1/2 tsp nutmeg
- 1 tsp turmeric
- 1 cup coconut milk
- 1 tbsp coconut oil

Instructions:

1. Sauté onion and garlic in coconut oil.
2. Add cloves, nutmeg, and turmeric.
3. Stir in breadfruit and coconut milk.
4. Simmer until breadfruit is tender.

Mascarene Island Cinnamon Sugar Plantains

Ingredients:

- 2 ripe plantains, sliced
- 2 tbsp butter
- 1 tbsp brown sugar
- 1 tsp cinnamon

Instructions:

1. Melt butter in a pan.
2. Add plantains and sprinkle with sugar and cinnamon.
3. Cook until caramelized, flipping once.

Black Lemongrass & Coconut Milk Soup

Ingredients:

- 2 stalks lemongrass, bruised
- 1 can coconut milk
- 3 cups vegetable broth
- 1 tsp black pepper
- 2 garlic cloves, minced
- 1 tsp ginger, grated

Instructions:

1. Sauté garlic and ginger.
2. Add lemongrass, coconut milk, and broth.
3. Simmer for 15 minutes, then strain and serve.

Sri Lankan Ceylon Pepper-Crusted Chicken

Ingredients:

- 2 chicken breasts
- 1 tbsp crushed Ceylon black pepper
- 1 tsp turmeric
- 1 tsp garlic powder
- 1 tbsp ghee

Instructions:

1. Rub chicken with pepper, turmeric, and garlic powder.
2. Sear in ghee until cooked through.

Goan Kokum & Clove Pickled Fish

Ingredients:

- 4 fish fillets
- 1 tbsp kokum extract
- 1/2 tsp cloves, ground
- 1 tsp mustard seeds
- 1 tsp red chili powder
- 2 tbsp vinegar

Instructions:

1. Marinate fish in kokum, cloves, and vinegar for 1 hour.
2. Pan-fry until cooked through.

Comorian Ginger & Nutmeg Banana Fritters

Ingredients:

- 2 ripe bananas, mashed
- 1 cup flour
- 1/2 tsp nutmeg
- 1/2 tsp ginger, grated
- 1 tbsp sugar
- 1/2 cup milk
- Oil for frying

Instructions:

1. Mix all ingredients into a batter.
2. Fry spoonfuls until golden brown.

Zanzibar Cinnamon & Mace Rice Pudding

Ingredients:

- 1/2 cup rice
- 2 cups coconut milk
- 1/2 tsp cinnamon
- 1/2 tsp mace
- 2 tbsp sugar

Instructions:

1. Cook rice in coconut milk until soft.
2. Stir in cinnamon, mace, and sugar.

Mauritian Fennel Seed & Saffron Lamb Curry

Ingredients:

- 1.5 lb lamb, cubed
- 1 tsp fennel seeds
- 1/2 tsp saffron, soaked in warm water
- 1 onion, chopped
- 3 garlic cloves, minced
- 1 tsp turmeric
- 1 cup coconut milk

Instructions:

1. Sauté onion, garlic, and fennel seeds.
2. Add lamb and turmeric.
3. Stir in saffron water and coconut milk.
4. Simmer for 1.5 hours.

Maldivian Pandan & Coconut Ice Cream

Ingredients:

- 1 cup coconut milk
- 1 cup heavy cream
- 1/2 cup sugar
- 4 pandan leaves, tied in a knot
- 4 egg yolks

Instructions:

1. Heat coconut milk, cream, sugar, and pandan leaves over low heat until fragrant.
2. Whisk egg yolks and slowly add the warm mixture.
3. Remove pandan leaves and churn in an ice cream maker.

Sri Lankan Tamarind & Aniseed Spiced Chutney

Ingredients:

- 1/2 cup tamarind pulp
- 1 tsp aniseed
- 1 tbsp jaggery
- 1/2 tsp chili powder
- 1/2 tsp ginger, grated

Instructions:

1. Heat tamarind pulp in a pan.
2. Stir in aniseed, jaggery, chili powder, and ginger.
3. Simmer until thick.

Kerala Black Sesame & Jaggery Sweet Porridge

Ingredients:

- 1/2 cup black sesame seeds, toasted
- 1/2 cup jaggery
- 1 cup coconut milk
- 1/2 cup rice flour

Instructions:

1. Grind sesame seeds into a paste.
2. Heat coconut milk and jaggery.
3. Stir in rice flour and sesame paste.
4. Cook until thickened.

Mascarene Island Vanilla Bean & Clove Cake

Ingredients:

- 1 cup flour
- 1/2 cup sugar
- 1 vanilla bean, scraped
- 1/2 tsp ground cloves
- 1/2 cup butter
- 2 eggs

Instructions:

1. Cream butter and sugar, then add eggs.
2. Mix in flour, vanilla, and cloves.
3. Bake at 350°F (175°C) for 30 minutes.

Andaman Islands Smoked Cumin & Cardamom Tea

Ingredients:

- 2 cups water
- 1/2 tsp smoked cumin seeds
- 2 green cardamom pods
- 1 tsp black tea leaves

Instructions:

1. Boil water with cumin and cardamom.
2. Add tea leaves and steep for 5 minutes.
3. Strain and serve.

Pondicherry Bay Leaf & Nutmeg Chicken Biryani

Ingredients:

- 2 cups basmati rice
- 1 lb chicken, cubed
- 2 bay leaves
- 1/2 tsp nutmeg
- 1 onion, sliced
- 1 tsp garam masala

Instructions:

1. Sauté onion with bay leaves.
2. Add chicken, nutmeg, and garam masala.
3. Layer with cooked rice and steam for 10 minutes.

Reunion Island Star Anise & Lemongrass Sorbet

Ingredients:

- 2 cups water
- 1/2 cup sugar
- 2 lemongrass stalks, bruised
- 2 star anise pods

Instructions:

1. Boil water with sugar, lemongrass, and star anise.
2. Strain, cool, and churn in an ice cream maker.

Mauritian Pink Pepper & Papaya Salad

Ingredients:

- 1 ripe papaya, sliced
- 1 tsp pink peppercorns, crushed
- 1 tbsp lime juice

Instructions:

1. Toss papaya slices with lime juice and pink pepper.

Zanzibar Cardamom & Clove-Spiced Mango Lassi

Ingredients:

- 1 cup yogurt
- 1 cup mango, chopped
- 1/2 tsp cardamom
- 1/4 tsp clove powder

Instructions:

1. Blend all ingredients until smooth.

Madagascar Vanilla & Cinnamon-Scented Roast Duck

Ingredients:

- 1 whole duck
- 1 vanilla bean, scraped
- 1 tsp cinnamon
- 1 tbsp honey

Instructions:

1. Rub duck with vanilla, cinnamon, and honey.
2. Roast at 375°F (190°C) for 1.5 hours.

www.ingramcontent.com/pod-product-compliance
Lightning Source LLC
LaVergne TN
LVHW081502060526
838201LV00056BA/2884